L'Wren Scott

Vera Wang

PLATE 1

Do not cut out space between arm and body.

PLATE 2   Azzedine Alaïa   Peter Soronen

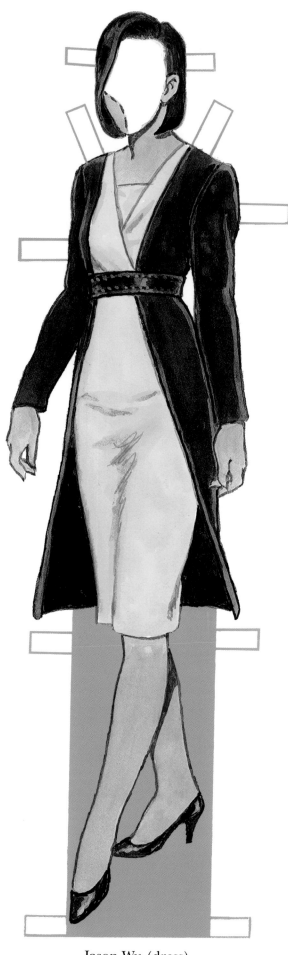

Jason Wu (dress)
Michael Kors (coat)

Marc Jacobs

PLATE 3

PLATE 4   Naeem Khan   Doo-Ri Chung

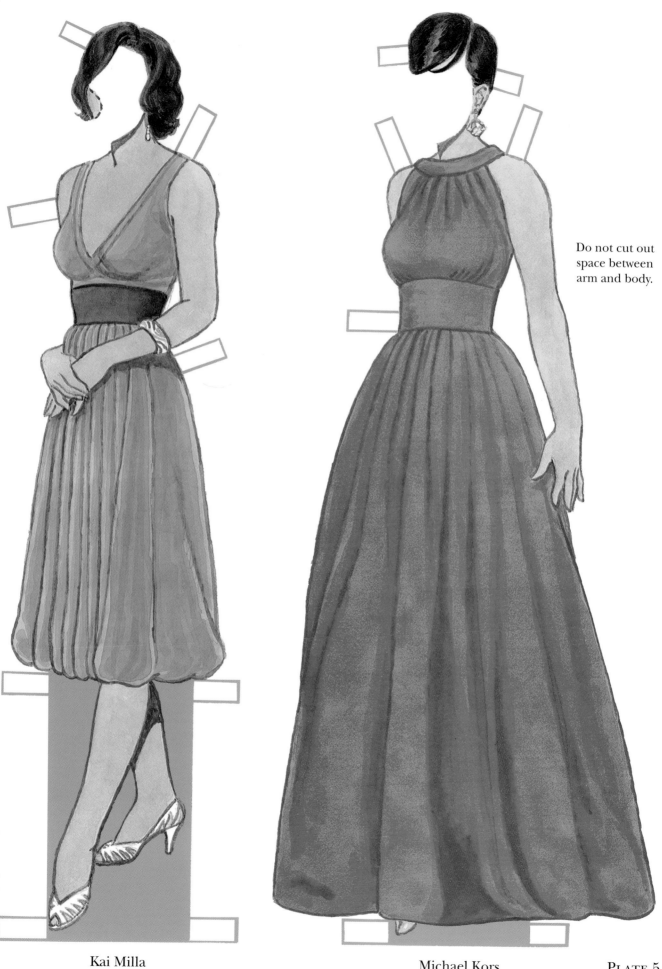

Do not cut out
space between
arm and body.

Kai Milla

Michael Kors

PLATE 5

Do not cut out space between arm and body.

PLATE 6   Thakoon Panichgul   House of Moschino

Ralph Lauren

Barbara Tfank

PLATE 7

PLATE 8   Sarah Burton for Alexander McQueen   Tom Ford

Do not cut out
space between
arm and body.

Peter Soronen

Marchesa

PLATE 9

Do not cut out
space between
arm and body.

PLATE 10   Jean Paul Gaultier   J. Mendel

Bibhu Mohapatra   Isabel Toledo   PLATE 11

PLATE 12   J. Mendel   Tracy Reese

Tracy Feith

Michael Kors

PLATE 13

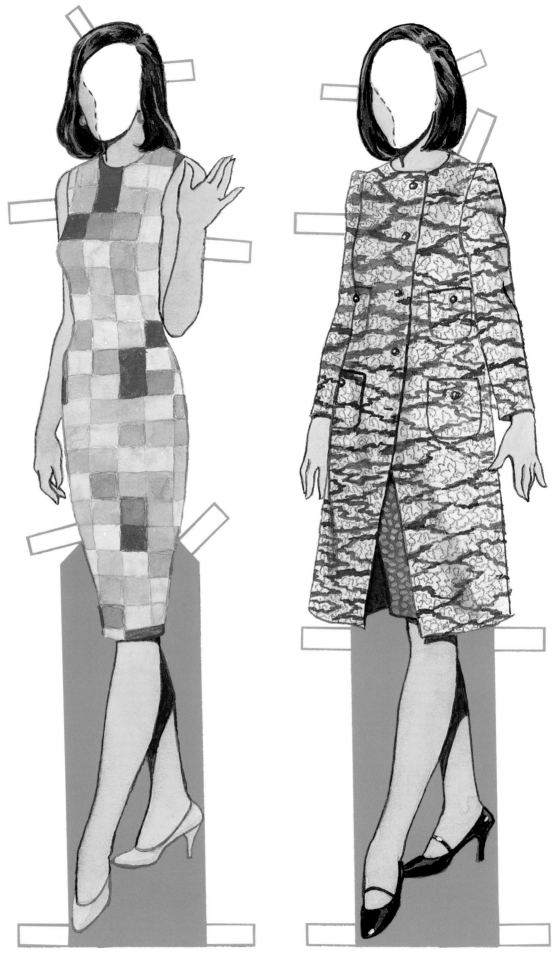

PLATE 14   Preen   Peter Som

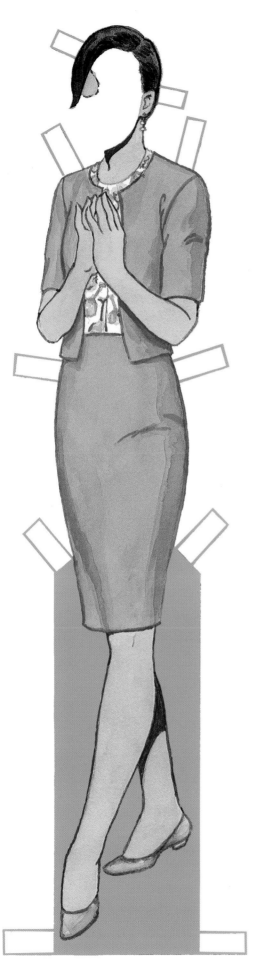

Narciso Rodriguez

Wes Gordon (blouse)
Helmut Lang (jeans)

PLATE 15

PLATE 16   Thom Browne   Jason Wu